PEANUTS™

Holiday Cookbook

PEANUTS™

Holiday Cookbook

SWEET TREATS FOR SPECIAL OCCASIONS ALL YEAR ROUND

weldon**owen**

CONTENTS

INTRODUCTION • 08

SPRING & SUMMER TREATS • 11

AUTUMN & WINTER TREATS • 59

INTRODUCTION

Gingerbread, sugar cookies, cupcakes, candy, pies, and cakes—deck the halls with the magical aromas of the holidays! With a pinch of fun, a dollop of love, and a heaping spoonful of *Peanuts* humor, young chefs can offer up treats for every occasion. From Valentine's Day, Mother's Day, and Easter through Halloween, Thanksgiving, Christmas, and more, these recipes will entice loved ones to celebrate a year's worth of holidays with festive sweets.

The delicious desserts presented here connect family and friends through year-round celebration, good food, the wit and whimsy of Charles M. Schulz, and the delightful characters he brought to the world.

Gather round the table and ring in the holidays with the *Peanuts* gang!

SPRING & SUMMER TREATS

ST. PATTY'S IRISH SODA BREAD

The aroma of this traditional rustic round loaf, best eaten warm from the oven, will attract leprechauns from far and wide.

INGREDIENTS

2¼ cups bread flour, plus flour for dusting

½ cup old-fashioned rolled oats

¼ cup wheat bran

1½ teaspoons baking soda

1 teaspoon salt

4 tablespoons cold unsalted butter, cut into 8 pieces

1½ cups plain low-fat yogurt

Makes 1 round loaf

1 Place a rimmed baking sheet in the oven and preheat the oven to 425°F.

2 In a large bowl, whisk together the flour, oats, wheat bran, baking soda, and salt. Scatter the butter pieces over the top. Using your fingers, rub the butter into the flour mixture until the mixture resembles coarse meal. Add the yogurt and quickly stir to blend the ingredients as evenly as possible, forming a rough ball.

3 Turn out the dough onto a lightly floured work surface and knead gently for about 30 seconds, dusting the dough with just enough flour to prevent it from sticking. The dough should feel soft. Form the dough into a ball and flatten the ball slightly into a dome. Sprinkle it with flour, spreading the flour lightly over the surface of the dough with your fingertips. Using a sharp knife, cut a shallow X on the top of the loaf.

4 Remove the baking sheet from the oven. Using a large metal spatula, transfer the loaf to the preheated baking sheet. Bake until the loaf is well risen, brown, and crusty and sounds hollow when tapped on the bottom, 30–35 minutes. Transfer the loaf to a wire rack to cool slightly, then serve warm.

LUCKY SHAMROCK COOKIES

These wee, green, clover-shaped confections will have you and all your friends dancing a jig on St. Patrick's Day!

INGREDIENTS

2½ cups all-purpose flour, plus flour for dusting

½ teaspoon baking powder

¼ teaspoon salt

1 cup unsalted butter, at room temperature

1 cup granulated sugar

1 large egg

2 teaspoons pure vanilla extract

½ teaspoon almond extract

Shamrock Icing (page 119)

Green sugar crystals for sprinkling (optional)

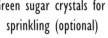

Makes 40 cookies

1 In a bowl, sift together the flour, baking powder, and salt.

2 In a large bowl, using an electric mixer, beat the butter and granulated sugar on medium speed until well blended, about 1 minute. Add the egg and vanilla and almond extracts and beat on low speed until blended. Beat in the flour mixture just until incorporated. Divide the dough in half and press each piece into a disk. Wrap each disk tightly in plastic wrap and refrigerate until firm, at least 1 hour or up to overnight.

3 Preheat the oven to 350°F. Line 3 large baking sheets with parchment paper.

4 Place 1 chilled dough disk on a floured work surface. Using a floured rolling pin, roll out the dough to about ¼-inch thick. Using a shamrock-shaped cookie cutter, cut out as many cookies as possible. Use a metal spatula to transfer the cookies to the prepared sheets, spacing them 1 inch apart. Press the dough scraps into a ball and refrigerate until firm. Repeat with the remaining chilled dough disk and scraps.

5 Bake, 1 sheet at a time, until the cookie bottoms and edges are lightly browned but the tops are barely colored, 10–13 minutes. Set the sheet on a wire rack to cool for 5 minutes, then transfer the cookies to the rack and let cool completely, about 30 minutes.

6 Pipe or drizzle the icing over the cookies, then sprinkle with the crystals, if using. Store in an airtight container at room temperature for up to 3 days.

SNOOPY'S POT O' GOLD

Make your very own pot of gold at the end of the rainbow this St. Patrick's Day. The homemade chocolate bowl will cradle your gold-dusted treasures!

INGREDIENTS

1 cup semisweet or bittersweet chocolate chips

1 tablespoon solid vegetable shortening

6 small balloons, such as those used for water balloons

1½ cups chocolate-covered raisins

¼–½ teaspoon edible gold luster dust

Makes 6 servings

1 In a microwave-safe bowl, combine the chocolate chips and shortening. Microwave on high power, stirring after 30 seconds, then after every 15 seconds, just until melted and smooth. Let the mixture cool until barely warm, 10–15 minutes. Meanwhile, blow up the balloons and knot each one at the end. Line a rimmed baking sheet with waxed paper.

2 When the chocolate has cooled, hold a balloon by the knotted end and dip it into the melted chocolate, covering about 3 inches of the balloon bottom. Place the chocolate-dipped balloon, chocolate side down, on the lined baking sheet. Repeat with the remaining balloons. Place the baking sheet in the refrigerator until the chocolate is set, 5–10 minutes. Pop the balloons with a pin and discard them. Set the chocolate cups aside at cool room temperature until ready to use, or refrigerate for up to 1 day.

3 Put the raisins in an airtight container. Add ¼ teaspoon of the gold dust, cover, and shake until evenly coated. If the color is too pale, add more gold dust and shake again until coated.

4 Divide the gold nuggets evenly among the chocolate cups and serve.

APRIL FOOL

Fool, an English dessert dating from the sixteenth century, swirls together cream and puréed fruit. It would be foolish indeed to pass up this delicious treat!

INGREDIENTS

1 cup blueberries

3 tablespoons sugar

1 tablespoon black currant syrup

1 cup heavy cream

½ teaspoon pure vanilla extract

¼ teaspoon finely grated lemon zest

Makes 4 servings

1 In a saucepan, combine the blueberries and 2 tablespoons of the sugar. Cook over medium heat, stirring often, until the berries are tender, about 10 minutes. Stir in the black currant syrup. Pour the berry mixture into a bowl and let cool, then cover and refrigerate for 1–2 hours.

2 In a large bowl, using an electric mixer, beat the cream, vanilla, and remaining 1 tablespoon sugar on medium speed until soft peaks form. Gently fold in the berry mixture and lemon zest with a silicone spatula.

3 Spoon the fool into dessert glasses and serve right away, or chill for up to 2 hours before serving.

WOODSTOCK'S EASTER EGG NEST

For a special Easter treat, make a coconut-covered meringue nest and fill it with colorful jelly beans.

INGREDIENTS

3 large egg whites, at room temperature

¼ teaspoon cream of tartar

Pinch of salt

¾ cup sugar

1 teaspoon pure vanilla extract

½ cup shredded dried coconut

1 bag (13 oz) large jelly beans, all different colors

Makes 12 nests

1 Preheat the oven to 225°F. Line 2 baking sheets with parchment paper.

2 In a large bowl, using an electric mixer, beat the egg whites on low speed until foamy. Add the cream of tartar and salt. Turn the mixer speed to high and beat until the whites stand in soft peaks. Beat in the sugar 1 tablespoon at a time. Occasionally stop the mixer and scrape down the sides of the bowl with a silicone spatula. Continue beating until the whites stand in stiff peaks (no droops), 15–20 minutes. Add the vanilla and beat until blended.

3 With a large spoon, drop 6 equal-size mounds of the mixture on each prepared baking sheet, leaving plenty of space between them. With the back of the spoon, make a depression in the center of each mound so that it looks like a little bird's nest. The nests don't have to be perfect. Sprinkle each nest with some coconut. Drop 3 jelly beans into the center of each nest.

4 Bake the nests for 2 hours. Turn off the oven, but leave the nests in the warm oven for 30 minutes.

5 Place the baking sheets on racks and let the nests cool completely.

6 With your fingers, carefully peel the paper from each nest. Add a few more jelly beans to the center of each nest and serve. Store in an airtight container at room temperature for up to 1 day.

"SIX BUNNY-WUNNIES" CARROT CUPCAKES

You—and the little Easter bunnies in your world—will do the happy dance when you taste these delightful cupcakes.

INGREDIENTS

2¼ cups all-purpose flour

1½ cups firmly packed golden brown sugar

1 tablespoon baking powder

1 teaspoon ground cinnamon

½ teaspoon salt

1½ cups grated carrots

¾ cup vegetable oil

4 large eggs, at room temperature, lightly beaten

1½ teaspoons pure vanilla extract

¾ cup finely chopped walnuts (optional)

1 recipe Cream Cheese Frosting (page 119)

Makes 18 cupcakes

1 Preheat the oven to 325°F. Line 18 standard muffin cups with paper liners.

2 In a large bowl, whisk together the flour, brown sugar, baking powder, cinnamon, and salt.

3 In a small bowl, combine the carrots, oil, eggs, and vanilla and stir until blended. Stir the carrot mixture into the flour mixture just until blended. Stir in the nuts, if using.

4 Pour the batter into the prepared muffin cups. Bake until a toothpick inserted into the center of a cupcake comes out clean, 16–18 minutes. Let cool in the pans on a wire rack for 5 minutes, then remove and let cool on the rack. Frost and serve, or store in an airtight container in the refrigerator for up to 3 days and frost just before serving.

CORMACAROONS

Craving coconut this spring? These sweet and chewy macaroons are perfect for Passover because there's no flour or leavening agents.

INGREDIENTS

3½ cups sweetened shredded coconut

¾ cup sugar

5 large egg whites, lightly beaten

1½ teaspoons pure vanilla extract

¼ teaspoon almond extract

Makes about 18 macaroons

1 Line a rimmed baking sheet with parchment paper. In a bowl, combine the coconut, sugar, egg whites, and vanilla and almond extracts and stir well. Spread on the prepared baking sheet and refrigerate until cold, about 30 minutes.

2 Preheat the oven to 300°F. Line another rimmed baking sheet with parchment paper.

3 Scoop up the coconut mixture by heaping tablespoonfuls and pack into small, rounded domes. Place on the prepared baking sheet.

4 Bake until the macaroons are golden, about 30 minutes. Transfer the macaroons to a rack and let cool completely.

5 Store in an airtight container in the refrigerator for up to 3 days. Let stand at room temperature for about 1 hour before serving.

EASTER EGG LOLLIPOPS

You can make these white-chocolate Easter egg lollies with your friends.
Make the plain lollipops ahead of time and decorate them when you are together.

INGREDIENTS

1 bag (11 oz) white chocolate chips

3 colors food coloring

Small candies and/or sprinkles for decorating (optional)

Makes 8 lollipops

1 Pour the chocolate chips into a heatproof bowl set over but not touching simmering water in a saucepan. Heat, stirring occasionally, until melted and smooth, about 5 minutes.

2 Divide half of the melted chocolate into 3 small bowls. Add 1 drop of food coloring to each and stir until blended. Spoon each batch of colored chocolate into a small lock-top plastic bag, press out the air, and seal. Place the filled portion of each bag in a small bowl of warm water so the chocolate doesn't harden.

3 Place lollipop sticks on a large sheet of waxed paper, several inches apart. For each lollipop, spoon a dollop of the plain white chocolate over one end of the stick, then use the spoon to spread the chocolate into an oval about 2 x 3 inches. Twist the stick gently to coat it with chocolate. The stick should extend from the middle of the oval. Carefully dry the bags of colored chocolate and snip off one corner. Pipe designs onto each oval, then decorate as desired. Let dry until firm, about 15 minutes. Peel away the waxed paper and enjoy!

LINUS'S LEMON DROP BARS

These sweet, tart, and melt-in-your-mouth Easter treats are perfect for lemon-loving siblings.

INGREDIENTS

FOR THE CRUST:

1¼ cups all-purpose flour

½ cup confectioners' sugar

¼ cup cornstarch

½ teaspoon salt

½ cup plus 3 tablespoons cold unsalted butter, cut into ½-inch pieces

1 tablespoon cold water

FOR THE FILLING:

3 large eggs plus 3 large egg yolks

1 cup granulated sugar

3 tablespoons all-purpose flour

½ teaspoon salt

1 tablespoon grated lemon zest

3/4 cup fresh lemon juice

1/3 cup whole milk

Confectioners' sugar for dusting

Makes 16 bars

1   To make the crust, lightly grease an 8-inch square baking pan. Line the pan with parchment paper, letting the paper overhang on two opposite sides by 2 inches.

2   In a food processor, combine the flour, confectioners' sugar, cornstarch, and salt and pulse until blended. Add the butter and pulse until the mixture is coarse and pale yellow, 8–10 pulses. Add the cold water and pulse 2–4 times, until just combined.

3   Sprinkle the mixture into the prepared pan and press firmly into an even layer ¼–½ inch thick over the bottom of the pan and about ½ inch up the sides. Refrigerate for 20 minutes. Meanwhile, preheat the oven to 350°F.

4   Bake until the crust is golden brown, 25–30 minutes. Remove the pan from the oven and reduce the oven temperature to 325°F.

5   To make the filling, in a bowl, whisk together the eggs, egg yolks, granulated sugar, flour, salt, lemon zest and juice, and milk until combined. Pour the filling on top of the warm crust.

6   Bake until the filling is just set and barely jiggles in the center, 25–30 minutes. Set the pan on a wire rack and let cool for 30 minutes. Use the parchment paper to lift the dessert from the dish. Cut into 16 bars and dust generously with confectioners' sugar.

JOSÉ PETERSON'S BUNDT CAKE

Forget about a late-game bunt! Sluggers will swing for the fences on Opening Day after trying this luscious lemony, blueberry Bundt cake.

INGREDIENTS

3 cups all-purpose flour

1 tablespoon baking powder

½ teaspoon salt

6 tablespoons unsalted butter, at room temperature

1/3 cups (11 oz/340 g) sugar

2 large eggs

2 teaspoons pure vanilla extract

1 teaspoon grated lemon zest

¼ cup sour cream

¾ cup milk

2 cups fresh or frozen blueberries

1 recipe Lemon Icing (page 119)

Makes 10 servings

1 Preheat the oven to 350°F. Grease a 10-inch Bundt pan. In a bowl, sift together the flour, baking powder, and salt.

2 In a large bowl, using an electric mixer, beat the butter on medium-high speed until light. Add the sugar and beat until blended. Add the eggs one at a time, beating well after each addition. Beat in the vanilla and lemon zest and then the sour cream. Reduce the speed to low and beat the flour mixture into the butter mixture alternately with the milk, beginning and ending with the flour mixture. Beat just until combined. The batter will be very thick.

3 Spoon half of the batter into the prepared pan. Scatter 1 cup of the blueberries over the batter. Gently press the berries into the batter. Spoon the remaining batter over the berries and then scatter the remaining berries over the top, again pressing them gently into the batter. Bake until a toothpick inserted near the center comes out clean, about 1 hour. Transfer to a rack and let cool in the pan for 10 minutes. Invert onto the rack and let cool completely.

4 Transfer the cake to a plate. Drizzle the icing evenly over the top, allowing it to run over the sides slightly. Serve immediately, or cover and store at room temperature for up to 1 day.

"PITCHER" OF FRUIT PUNCH

Help your team's pitcher cool off on the mound with a glass of this refreshing, sparkling, fruit-filled juice.

INGREDIENTS

1 lemon, thinly sliced,
   with peel
1 orange, thinly sliced,
   with peel
1 lime, thinly sliced,
   with peel
1 apple, cored and chopped
8 strawberries
¼ cup fresh lemon juice
1 cup fresh orange juice
3 cups red grape juice
1 (25.4-oz) bottle
   sparkling apple cider
   or sparkling water

Makes 6 to 8 servings

1 Layer the fruit in the bottom of a large glass pitcher. Pour in the lemon, orange, and grape juices and gently stir. Refrigerate at least 3 hours.

2 Serve over ice with sparkling cider or sparkling water to taste.

PIGPEN'S DIRT CAKE

For a special Earth Day treat, try this double-layer chocolate cake with a sprinkling of dusty "dirt" crumbs that would make Pigpen proud.

INGREDIENTS

4 oz unsweetened chocolate, finely chopped

2¼ cups all-purpose flour

1 teaspoon baking soda

¼ teaspoon salt

1 cup unsalted butter, at room temperature

1 cup firmly packed golden brown sugar

¾ cup granulated sugar

4 large eggs, at room temperature

2 teaspoons pure vanilla extract

1 cup low-fat buttermilk, at room temperature

1 recipe Chocolate Fudge Frosting (page 120)

Sweetened cocoa powder, for dusting

Makes 10 to 12 servings

1 Preheat the oven to 350°F. Grease two 9-inch round cake pans. Line the cake pans with parchment paper cut to fit the bottom exactly. Grease the paper and then sprinkle lightly with flour, tapping out the excess.

2 Put the unsweetened chocolate in a heatproof bowl set over but not touching simmering water in a saucepan. Heat, stirring often, until melted and smooth, about 5 minutes. Remove from the heat and let cool.

3 In a bowl, whisk together the flour, baking soda, and salt.

4 In a large bowl, using a handheld mixer or a stand mixer fitted with the paddle attachment, beat together the butter and both sugars on medium speed until creamy, about 2 minutes. Add the eggs one at a time, beating well after each addition. Stop the mixer and scrape down the sides of the bowl with a silicone spatula. Add the vanilla and beat on medium speed for 1 minute longer. Add the melted chocolate and beat until evenly blended. With the mixer on low speed, add the flour mixture alternately with the buttermilk, beginning and ending with the flour mixture and beating just until blended after each addition. Stop the mixer and scrape down the sides of the bowl with the spatula as needed.

CONTINUED on page 35 . . .

... CONTINUED from page 33

5 Pour the batter into the prepared pans, dividing it evenly. Bake until a toothpick inserted into the center of each cake comes out clean, 30–35 minutes. Transfer the cakes to wire racks and let cool in the pans for 20 minutes. Invert 1 cake layer onto a plate, lift off the pan, peel off the parchment paper, and turn the layer right-side up. Repeat with the other cake layer. Let the cakes cool completely.

6 Use a serrated knife to slice off the rounded top from each cake layer. Working over a plate, force the trimmed pieces of cake through a coarse-mesh sieve to make crumbs; set aside.

7 Place a cake layer, bottom side down, on a cake plate. Scoop about one-third of the frosting onto the center and, using an icing spatula, spread the frosting evenly over the top. Place the second cake layer, top side down, on top. Spread frosting around the sides of the cake, then frost the top. Scatter the chocolate cake crumbs over the frosted cake, using your hands to press the crumbs against the top and sides. Dust with cocoa powder. Cut into wedges and serve.

LUCY'S ARBOR DAY CUPCAKES

These sweet cakes are perfect for a picnic under a tree at your favorite park.

INGREDIENTS

1¼ cups all-purpose flour

1¼ teaspoons baking powder

¼ teaspoon salt

6 tablespoons unsalted butter,
   at room temperature

¾ cup sugar

2 large eggs

1 teaspoon pure vanilla extract

1/3 cup whole milk

1 recipe Vanilla Frosting
   (page 120)

Pretzel Trees for decorating
   (page 120)

Makes 12 cupcakes

1 Preheat the oven to 350°F. Line a standard 12-cup muffin pan with paper or foil liners.

2 In a small bowl, whisk together the flour, baking powder, and salt. In a large bowl, using an electric mixer, beat the butter and sugar on medium-high speed until light and fluffy, 2–3 minutes. Add the eggs one at a time, beating well after each addition. Turn off the mixer and scrape down the bowl with a silicone spatula. Add the vanilla and beat until combined. Add about half of the flour mixture and mix on low speed just until blended. Add the milk and mix on low speed until combined. Add the remaining flour mixture and mix just until blended. Turn off the mixer, scrape down the bowl, and give the batter a final stir with the spatula.

3 Divide the batter evenly among the prepared muffin cups. Bake until the tops are light golden brown and a toothpick inserted into the center of a cupcake comes out clean, 18–20 minutes. Remove the pan from the oven and set it on a wire rack. Let cool for 10 minutes, then carefully transfer the cupcakes directly to the rack. Let cool completely, about 1 hour.

4 Using a small icing spatula or a butter knife, top the cupcakes with the frosting. Plant a pretzel tree on top of each cupcake and enjoy!

WOODSTOCK'S CHURRO CHÜRPS

These fried-dough pastries, originally from Spain, are perfect for Cinco de Mayo!

INGREDIENTS

FOR THE CHOCOLATE SAUCE:

1 cup half-and-half

3 tablespoons unsalted butter,
  cut into ½-inch cubes

½ cup granulated sugar

⅓ cup unsweetened
  cocoa powder

1 teaspoon pure vanilla extract

FOR THE CHURROS:

1 cup water

½ cup unsalted butter

½ teaspoon salt

1 cup all-purpose flour

3 large eggs, at room
  temperature

½ teaspoon pure vanilla extract

Canola oil for deep-frying

⅔ cup granulated sugar

1 teaspoon ground cinnamon

Makes about 35 churros

1. To make the chocolate sauce, combine the half-and-half, butter, sugar, and cocoa powder in a saucepan and bring to a simmer over medium-low heat, whisking to dissolve the sugar and cocoa powder. Cook for 1 minute, whisking constantly. Remove from the heat and stir in the vanilla. Pour the sauce into a heatproof bowl, cover, and set aside.

2. To make the churros, combine the water, butter, and salt in a saucepan and bring to a boil over medium heat, stirring to melt the butter. Add the flour all at once and stir vigorously with a wooden spoon until the flour is incorporated and the dough pulls away from the sides of the pan in a ball. Reduce the heat to low and cook, stirring constantly, for 1 minute. The dough will continue to pull away from the pan sides in a large clump.

3. Scrape the dough into a large bowl. Using an electric mixer set (use the paddle attachment for a stand mixer), beat on medium speed until the dough forms large clumps, about 1 minute. Add the eggs one at a time, beating until smooth after each addition. Beat in the vanilla.

CHÜRP

4 Line a rimmed baking sheet with paper towels. Pour oil to a depth of 2 inches into a deep-fryer or deep, heavy sauté pan and heat over medium-high heat until it reads 360°F on a deep-frying thermometer.

5 Fit a pastry bag with a ½-inch star tip and spoon the dough into the bag. Dip a large, wide metal spatula into the hot oil, letting any excess drip back into the fryer. Pipe 2 dough strips, each 6–7 inches long, onto the spatula, spacing them about 1 inch apart. Slide the spatula into the hot oil and let the dough strips slide off into the oil. Repeat to add 2–4 more strips to the oil, taking care not to crowd the pan. The churros will expand and float to the top. Deep-fry until dark golden on the first side, about 2 minutes. Using tongs, a wire skimmer, or a slotted spoon, turn and fry until dark golden on the second side, about 1½ minutes longer. Transfer to the lined baking sheet to drain. Repeat to fry the remaining churros, allowing the oil to return to 360°F between batches.

6 In a large, shallow bowl, whisk together the sugar and cinnamon. When the churros are cool enough to handle, roll them in the cinnamon-sugar to coat generously. (You may have extra cinnamon-sugar, but this makes for easier coating.) Arrange the churros on a platter and serve right away with the warm chocolate sauce for dipping.

MOTHER'S DAY MANGO SMOOTHIE

Delight your mother with breakfast in bed featuring a fruity smoothie. It is so easy to prepare, you may be able to make it without her help!

INGREDIENTS

1 cup ice cubes

2 bananas, peeled

4 cups fresh or thawed frozen mango cubes

¾ cup low-fat vanilla yogurt

1 cup fresh orange juice

¼ cup whole milk

Makes 3 to 4 servings

1 Put the ice in a blender. Break each banana into quarters and add to the blender. Add the mango, yogurt, orange juice, and milk and process until smooth.

2 Divide the mixture evenly among 3 or 4 glasses and serve.

VARIATIONS: For a thicker smoothie, use frozen mango cubes or add more ice. For a smoothie more akin to a milkshake, use half-and-half instead of milk.

SPIKE'S CHOCOLATE-DIPPED WAFFLES

Say "I love you" with delicious warm waffles and a side of chocolate sauce on Mother's Day morning!

INGREDIENTS

2 large eggs

1½ cups buttermilk, plus buttermilk as needed

½ cup unsalted butter, melted, or ½ cup canola oil

1½ cups all-purpose flour

2 tablespoons sugar

2 teaspoons baking powder

1 teaspoon baking soda

¼ teaspoon salt

1 recipe Chocolate Sauce (page 38)

Makes 4 to 8 waffles

1 To make the waffles, in a medium bowl, whisk together the eggs, buttermilk, and butter.

2 In a large bowl, whisk together the flour, sugar, baking powder, baking soda, and salt. Make a well in the center of the dry ingredients, then pour in the egg mixture. Whisk until mostly smooth, with just a few lumps. If the batter seems too thick, stir in another 1–2 tablespoons buttermilk.

3 Preheat a waffle maker. Ladle the batter into the waffle maker, using ½–¾ cup batter per batch. Spread the batter so that it almost reaches the edges of the waffle maker. Cook until the waffles are crisp and browned, 3–4 minutes.

4 Using a spatula, remove the waffles from the waffle maker and serve right away, or place in a single layer on a baking sheet in a 200°F oven to keep warm for up to 20 minutes before serving with warm chocolate sauce for dipping.

Panel 1: "SNICKER-SNACKS" GIVE ME LOTS OF ENERGY..

Panel 2: "SNICKER-SNACKS" ARE HELPING ME TO GROW INTO A STRONG, HEALTHY ADULT!

Panel 3: "SNICKER-SNACKS" ARE GIVING LITTLE KIDS ALL OVER THE WORLD A BETTER WAY OF LIFE...

Panel 4: I TELL YOU, THE PEOPLE WHO MAKE "SNICKER-SNACKS" ARE GREAT HUMANITARIANS!

CHARLIE BROWN'S SUMMERTIME SNICKER-SNACKS

These granola bars are healthy snacks for all your summer holiday adventures!

INGREDIENTS

1 cup hazelnuts

½ cup wheat germ

1 teaspoon ground cinnamon

½ teaspoon salt

2½ cups old-fashioned rolled oats

1 cup dried cranberries

½ cup pecans, chopped

½ cup unsalted butter, cut into pieces

½ cup firmly packed golden brown sugar

½ cup all-natural peanut butter

⅓ cup maple syrup

2 large egg whites, lightly beaten

Makes 12 bars

1 Preheat the oven to 350°F. Grease a 9 × 13-inch baking pan.

2 Spread the hazelnuts on a rimmed baking sheet and bake until lightly toasted, about 10 minutes. Wrap the hazelnuts in a clean kitchen towel and let cool slightly, about 1 minute, then rub the nuts in the towel to remove the loose skins. Some specks of skin will remain. Leave the oven on.

3 In a food processor, combine the toasted hazelnuts, wheat germ, cinnamon, and salt and pulse just until finely ground, about 20 short pulses. Transfer to a bowl and stir in the oats, cranberries, and pecans.

4 In a small saucepan, combine the butter, brown sugar, peanut butter, and maple syrup over medium heat, bring to a simmer, and cook for 1 minute, stirring constantly. Pour the peanut butter mixture evenly over the oat mixture, stir to combine, and let cool for 5 minutes.

5 Add the egg whites to the granola mixture and stir well. Press the mixture into the prepared baking pan, packing it down with a silicone spatula. Bake until golden brown around the edges and no longer sticky to the touch, 20–25 minutes. Cut into 12 bars in the pan, then let cool for at least 1 hour.

6 Wrap the bars individually in plastic wrap. Store in an airtight container at room temperature for up to 10 days.

SPIKE'S FATHER'S DAY MARSHMALLOWS

Once you try homemade marshmallows, you'll agree that they're the best!

INGREDIENTS

½ cup confectioners' sugar

¼ cup cornstarch

1 cup water

1½ tablespoons powdered
   unflavored gelatin

¼ teaspoon salt

¼ teaspoon cream of tartar

1¼ cups granulated sugar

1 tablespoon light corn syrup

1 teaspoon pure vanilla
   extract

Makes one 9 X 11-inch
   sheet, about
   30 marshmallows

1 In a bowl, sift together the confectioners' sugar and cornstarch. Line a 9 x 11-inch baking pan with aluminum foil and lightly grease the foil. Sift ¼ cup of the sugar-starch mixture into the pan and tilt to coat the bottom and sides. Leave any excess evenly in the bottom.

2 Pour ½ cup of the water into the bowl of a stand mixer. Sprinkle the gelatin over the water, gently whisk, then let stand for 5 minutes to soften. Whisk in the salt and cream of tartar, then beat on high speed until fluffy, 2–3 minutes.

3 Pour the remaining ½ cup water into a saucepan. Stir in the granulated sugar and corn syrup. Bring to a boil over medium-high heat, then cook, without stirring, until the mixture turns pale tan (about 250°F on a candy thermometer).

4 With the mixer on medium speed, carefully drizzle the hot sugar syrup into the gelatin mixture, aiming it between the beater and the side of the bowl. Increase the speed to high and whip the mixture until it is white and thick, about 5 minutes. Add the vanilla and beat until the mixture cools, about 20 minutes.

5 Pour the mixture into the prepared pan. Dip an offset spatula in cold water and smooth the surface. Let stand until a skin forms on the surface, about 1 hour. Dust with ¼ cup of the sugar-starch mixture and let rest overnight at cool room temperature.

6 Line a rimmed baking sheet with parchment paper and dust with the remaining sugar-starch mixture. Dip a knife into the remaining sugar-starch mixture and cut out 1½–2 inch squares. Layer the squares in the pan, dusting with more of the sugar-starch mixture. Cover tightly and store at room temperature for up to 2 weeks.

Dear Dad, Thinking of you on Father's Day.

Yesterday I created a new recipe.

I called it "Toasted Marshmallows on a Cactus."

It didn't work out so well...

I'm wondering if I couldn't try the same thing with hot dogs.

Anyway, Happy Father's Day. Your loving son, Spike

P.S. Please send me some hot dogs.

CHARLIE BROWN'S (UN)HAPPY BIRTHDAY CAKE

This cake is so good, all your friends will want a seat at the table!

INGREDIENTS

2 cups all-purpose flour, plus flour for dusting

1 tablespoon baking powder

¼ teaspoon salt

¾ cup unsalted butter, at room temperature

1¾ cup sugar

2 teaspoons pure vanilla extract

3 large eggs, at room temperature

1⅓ cups whole milk, at room temperature

1 recipe Vanilla Frosting (page 120)

4 containers (about 12 oz total) nonpareil rainbow sprinkles

Makes 10 to 12 servings

1 Preheat the oven to 350°F. Grease two 8- or 9-inch round cake pans and dust with flour, tapping out the excess. In a bowl, whisk together the flour, baking powder, and salt.

2 In a large bowl, using a handheld mixer or a stand mixer fitted with the paddle attachment, beat together the butter, sugar, and vanilla on medium speed until creamy, about 3 minutes. Add the eggs one at a time, beating well after each addition. Turn off the mixer and scrape down the sides of the bowl with a silicone spatula. With the mixer on low speed, add the flour mixture alternately with the milk, beginning and ending with the flour mixture and beating just until blended after each addition. Scrape down the bowl with the spatula.

3 Pour the batter into the prepared pans, dividing it evenly. Bake until golden and a toothpick inserted into the center of each cake comes out clean, 30–35 minutes. Transfer the cakes to wire racks and let cool in the pans for 20 minutes. Invert the cakes onto plates, lift off the pans, and invert again onto the racks. Let cool completely.

4 Place a cake layer, bottom side down, on a cake plate. Scoop about one-third of the frosting onto the center and, using an icing spatula, spread the frosting evenly over the top. Place the second cake layer, top side down, on top. Using an offset spatula, smooth the frosting over the top and sides of the cake. Pour the sprinkles into a bowl. Using your hand, scoop the sprinkles onto the sides of the cake, gently pressing them into the frosting, then sprinkle them over the top to cover the cake completely.

WORRY-FREE SUNDAE

Celebrate the end of the school year with a classic ice-cream sundae. The only thing you'll worry about is whether you can have another helping!

INGREDIENTS

FOR THE ICE CREAM:

2 cups cold heavy cream

1 cup cold whole milk

3/4 cup sugar, preferably superfine

1 tablespoon pure vanilla extract

Chocolate syrup

Whipped cream

Chopped toasted nuts, such as almonds, peanuts, or pecans (optional)

Maraschino cherries (optional)

Makes 1 pint

1 To make the ice-cream base, in a large bowl, whisk together the cream and milk. Add the sugar and whisk until completely dissolved, 3–4 minutes. Stir in the vanilla. Cover and refrigerate for at least 3 hours or up to 24 hours.

2 To freeze the ice cream, pour the ice cream base into an ice cream maker and freeze according to the manufacturer's instructions. Transfer to a freezer-safe container and freeze until firm, at least 3 hours or up to 3 days.

3 To prepare the sundae, place 2–3 scoops of ice cream in a bowl and top with the chocolate sauce, whipped cream, and nuts and cherries, if using.

VARIATIONS

Banana Split: Split a banana lengthwise. Place the banana slices along the sides of a long, narrow dish. Place 3 scoops of ice cream in between the bananas and top with chocolate sauce, whipped cream, and nuts and cherries, if using.

Mint Chip: Substitute 1½ teaspoons peppermint extract for the vanilla. Add ¾ cup semisweet chocolate chips to the ice cream maker during the last 5 minutes of freezing time.

Cookies & Cream: Add ¾ cup coarsely chopped Oreos to the ice cream maker during the last 5 minutes of freezing time.

SCHROEDER'S PIANO KEY LIME PIE

Key limes make exceptionally sweet music when mixed with sugar, graham crackers, and cream. Enjoy this pie at your Fourth of July extravaganza!

INGREDIENTS

1¼ cups graham cracker crumbs

5 tablespoons unsalted butter, melted

3 tablespoons sugar

7 large egg yolks

4 teaspoons finely grated Key lime zest

2 cans (14 oz each) sweetened condensed milk

1 cup fresh Key lime juice, strained (about 24 limes; see Note)

Whipped Cream for serving

Makes 6 to 8 servings

1 Preheat the oven to 350°F.

2 In a bowl, stir together the crumbs, melted butter, and sugar until evenly moistened. Pat the crumb mixture firmly and evenly into the bottom and all the way up the sides of a 9-inch pie pan. Bake until the crust is firm, 5–7 minutes.

3 In a bowl, whisk together the egg yolks and lime zest until well mixed. Whisk in the condensed milk and then the lime juice. Pour the filling into the crust.

4 Bake until the filling is firm in the center, 20–24 minutes. Transfer to a wire rack and let the pie cool completely. Refrigerate until chilled and firm, 2–3 hours.

5 Spread the top of the pie with a thick layer of whipped cream and serve.

NOTE: Look for key limes in well-stocked markets, sometimes labeled Mexican or West Indian limes. You can substitute Persian limes, but they will produce a more tart pie.

FLYING ACE ROCKET POPS

Cool down on Independence Day with these classic red-white-and-blue firecracker pops.

INGREDIENTS

1 teaspoon finely grated
  lemon zest

$^{1}/_{2}$ cup freshly squeezed
  lemon juice (from about
  4 lemons)

$^{1}/_{2}$ cup plus 2 tablespoons
  superfine sugar

Pinch of salt

1$^{3}/_{4}$ cups water

Blue and red food coloring

Makes 6 to 8 ice pops

1 In a pitcher, combine the lemon zest and juice, sugar, and salt. Pour in the water and stir to dissolve the sugar. Pour some of the lemonade into two smaller pitchers, dividing it evenly among the three pitchers. Stir 3 drops of blue food coloring into the first pitcher, stir 3 drops of red food coloring into the second pitcher, and leave the mixture in the third pitcher uncolored.

2 Divide the red lemonade among 6–8 ice-pop molds or plastic cups, filling them one-third of the way. Freeze until partially frozen, about 1 hour. If using sticks, insert them at this point. Carefully pour the uncolored lemonade into the ice-pop molds, dividing the mixture evenly over the red layer. Freeze until partially frozen, about 1 hour.

3 Pour the blue lemonade mixture over the uncolored layer, dividing it evenly. Cover and freeze until solid, at least 3 hours or up to 3 days.

LUCY'S PEACH CLOBBER

This peachy sweet cobbler, perfect for a Fourth of July picnic, is sure to pacify even your surliest guests!

INGREDIENTS

6 tablespoons unsalted butter, plus more for the baking dish

5 lbs peaches

1/2 cup firmly-packed golden brown sugar

2 tablespoons cornstarch

3/4 cup half-and-half

1 large egg

1 teaspoon pure vanilla extract

2 cups all-purpose flour

1/4 cup granulated sugar, plus more for sprinkling

1 tablespoon baking powder

1/2 teaspoon fine sea salt

Vanilla ice cream for serving

Makes 8 servings

1 Preheat the oven to 375°F. Lightly butter a 9 x 13-inch baking dish. Have ready a bowl of ice water.

2 Bring a large pot of water to a boil over high heat. A few at a time, plunge the peaches into the boiling water just until the skins loosen, about 1 minute. Using a slotted spoon, transfer to the bowl of ice water. Peel, pit, and slice the peaches; you should have about 12 cups.

3 In a bowl, toss together the peaches, brown sugar, and cornstarch. Spread in the prepared baking dish, place the dish on a baking sheet, and bake for 15 minutes.

4 Meanwhile, in a bowl, whisk together the half-and-half, egg, and vanilla until well blended. In another bowl, sift together the flour, the 1/4 cup granulated sugar, baking powder, and salt. Cut the butter into tablespoons and scatter over the flour mixture. Using a pastry blender or 2 knives, cut the butter into the flour mixture just until the mixture forms coarse crumbs the size of peas. Add the half-and-half mixture and stir just until the dough comes together.

5 When the filling has baked for 15 minutes, remove it from the oven. Drop the dough onto the filling in 8 heaping, evenly spaced spoonfuls. Return to the oven and bake until the peach juices are bubbling, the topping is golden brown, and a toothpick inserted into the topping comes out clean, 30–40 minutes more.

6 Transfer to a wire rack and let cool for at least 30 minutes. Serve warm with scoops of ice cream.

Panel 1: WHAT ARE YOU EATING FOR LUNCH, EUDORA?

Panel 2: THIS IS A CHOCOLATE SANDWICH

Panel 3: I PUT A CHOCOLATE BAR BETWEEN TWO SLICES OF DARK BREAD

Panel 4: I OFTEN WONDER HOW IT WOULD TASTE WITH GRAVY ON IT...

EUDORA'S ADORABLE S'MORAS

Find the perfect stick and roast marshmallows over a campfire for the time-honored summer holiday tradition of making s'mores.

INGREDIENTS

8 graham crackers, broken into squares

1 bar (about 4.4-oz) milk chocolate, broken into 8 pieces

8 large marshmallows, homemade (see page 44) or store-bought

Makes 8 servings

1 Cover one of the graham cracker halves with chocolate pieces to fit your graham cracker. Skewer your marshmallows and toast them over an open flame until dark golden brown. Squish a hot marshmallow onto chocolate using a second piece of graham cracker.

NOTE: You can also make s'mores under the broiler. Just place 8 graham cracker squares on a baking sheet, top each one with a marshmallow, and broil for 5–10 minutes, watching them carefully so they don't burn. Put the other half of the graham cracker on top, slip in a piece of chocolate, and serve.

AUTUMN & WINTER TREATS

Panel 1: YOU HAVE THE LEAD IN A STAGE PLAY?

Panel 2: THAT'S GREAT... MAY I SEE THE PROGRAM?

Panel 3: HMM... "DR. BEAGLE...

Panel 4: ... AND MR. HYDE"

MONSTER CRISPIES

Create a monster menagerie for Halloween and enjoy sweet and spooky monster treats with edible eyeballs!

INGREDIENTS

5 tablespoons unsalted butter

1 lb marshmallows, homemade (see page 44) or store-bought

½ teaspoon pure vanilla extract

6 cups crispy rice cereal

1½ cups candy melts, in 3 colors of ½ cup each

3 teaspoons canola oil

2 tablespoons candy eyeballs or mini M&M's candies

Makes about 10 bars

1 Place a rack in the upper third of the oven and preheat to 375°F. Grease an 8-inch square baking dish, then line the bottom with parchment paper and grease the parchment. Line a rimmed baking sheet with parchment paper.

2 In a large saucepan, melt the butter over medium heat. Add the marshmallows and stir until melted, about 2 minutes. Remove the pan from the heat and stir in the vanilla. Add the crispy rice cereal and stir until well coated. Transfer the mixture to the prepared baking dish and spread in an even layer about ½ inch thick, pressing down to compact slightly. Let stand until set, about 15 minutes.

3 Meanwhile, put the candy melts in 3 microwave-safe bowls. Add 1 teaspoon canola oil to each bowl. Working with one bowl at time, microwave on high power, stirring after 30 seconds, then after every 15 seconds, just until melted and smooth.

4 Cut the rice cereal mixture into rectangular bars. Dip a short side of each bar into one of the colors, covering about 1 inch. Press a few candy eyeballs into the melted coating, then place the bar on the prepared baking sheet and let stand until set, about 15 minutes. Store in an airtight container at room temperature for up to 2 days.

WITCH HAT COOKIES

Chocolate kisses sit atop chocolate cookies to make these adorable Halloween treats. Pointy witch hats have never been so yummy!

INGREDIENTS

2¹/₄ cups all-purpose flour, plus flour for dusting

¹/₃ cup unsweetened cocoa powder

¹/₂ teaspoon baking powder

¹/₂ teaspoon baking soda

¹/₄ teaspoon salt

³/₄ cup unsalted butter, at room temperature

1 cup firmly packed light brown sugar

¹/₄ cup granulated sugar

1 large egg

1 teaspoon pure vanilla extract

1 cup Vanilla Frosting (page 120)

2–3 drops orange food coloring

30 chocolate kisses

Makes about 30 cookies

1 In a medium bowl, whisk together the flour, cocoa powder, baking powder, baking soda, and salt. In a large bowl, using an electric mixer, beat the butter and both sugars on medium-high speed until light and fluffy, 2–3 minutes. Add the egg and vanilla and beat on low speed until completely incorporated. Slowly add the flour mixture and continue to beat on low speed until just incorporated, scraping down the sides of the bowl as needed.

2 Press the dough into a rectangle, wrap tightly in plastic wrap, and refrigerate until firm, at least 1 hour or up to overnight.

3 Preheat the oven to 350°F. Line 2 baking sheets with parchment paper. On a floured work surface, roll out the dough about ¹/₈ inch thick. Using 2- to 3-inch round cookie cutters, cut out as many rounds as possible and transfer to the prepared baking sheets, spacing them about 1 inch apart. Gather up the dough scraps, reroll, and cut out additional rounds.

4 Bake until the cookies are firm to the touch, 12–15 minutes. Set the sheet on a wire rack to cool for 5 minutes, then transfer the cookies to the rack and let cool completely.

5 In a small bowl, stir the frosting and food coloring together until blended. Spoon the frosting into a piping bag with a ¹/₄-inch plain tip. Holding the bag over each cookie, pipe a quarter-size dollop of frosting over each cookie, then press a chocolate kiss on top.

PUMPKIN SPICE BARS

There's more than one way to celebrate the pumpkins of fall. Chock-full of cinnamon and ginger, these pumpkin bars are better than candy!

INGREDIENTS

1½ cups all-purpose flour

1 cup firmly packed golden brown sugar

½ cup granulated sugar

2 teaspoons baking powder

¼ teaspoon baking soda

2 teaspoons finely chopped crystallized ginger or ½ teaspoon ground ginger

1 teaspoon ground cinnamon

¼ teaspoon salt

2 large eggs

1 cup canned pumpkin purée

¾ cup raisins

½ cup vegetable oil

3 oz white chocolate, chopped

1 teaspoon solid vegetable shortening

Makes about 48 bars

1 In a large mixing bowl, whisk together the flour, both sugars, baking powder, baking soda, ginger, cinnamon, and salt.

2 In another mixing bowl, beat the eggs slightly. Stir in the pumpkin, raisins, and oil. Stir the pumpkin mixture into the flour mixture.

3 Spread the batter in a 10 × 15-inch baking pan. Bake until a toothpick inserted near the center comes out clean, about 15–20 minutes. Cool in the pan on a rack.

4 To make the topping, combine the white chocolate and shortening in a small lock-top plastic bag. Press out the air and seal the bag, then place the bag in a bowl of warm water until the contents are melted. Snip ¼ inch from one corner of the bag. Squeeze the topping over the bars in a crisscross design. Cut into 1½ × 2-inch bars before the topping is completely set. Store in an airtight container in the refrigerator for up to 3 days.

BOO-NILLA GHOST MILKSHAKES

Make your milkshake spooky and delicious with a chocolate ghost-face.

INGREDIENTS

1½ cups vanilla ice cream

¾ cup whole milk

2 tablespoons chocolate sauce

Whipped cream for serving
  (optional)

2 maraschino cherries for
  serving (optional)

Makes 2 servings

1 Place two 16-oz glasses in the freezer until chilled, about 5 minutes.

2 In a blender, combine the ice cream and milk and blend until smooth.

3 Remove the glasses from the freezer. Dip your fingertip into the chocolate and draw a ghost face—two round eyes and an oblong mouth—on the inside of each chilled glass.

4 Divide the milkshake between the two glasses. Garnish each milkshake with whipped cream and a maraschino cherry, if using, and serve.

"PEANUTS" — DO YOUR MOM AND DAD EAT MUCH CANDY?

NO, THEY DON'T...AND THEY HARDLY EVER EAT ICE CREAM..

AND I ALMOST NEVER SEE THEM EATING POPCORN OR POTATO CHIPS..

I DON'T KNOW HOW THEY STAY ALIVE!

LUCY'S TASTY TOFFEE

You will be tempted to use all your tricks to taste these delectable walnut-orange toffee treats on Halloween night!

INGREDIENTS

1¼ cups unsalted butter

1 cup granulated sugar

¼ cup firmly packed golden brown sugar

¼ cup water

1 tablespoon dark molasses (not blackstrap)

1 cup coarsely chopped walnuts, plus ½ cup medium-fine chopped walnuts

1 tablespoon grated orange zest

6 oz semisweet chocolate, finely chopped

Makes about 1½ lb candy

1 Grease a small rimmed baking sheet and set aside. In a small, heavy saucepan, melt the butter over low heat. Add both sugars, the water, and the molasses and stir until the sugars dissolve, about 5 minutes. Raise the heat to medium and clip a candy thermometer onto the side of the pan. Cook, stirring slowly but constantly, until the thermometer registers 290°F, about 15 minutes.

2 Remove the pan from the heat. Stir in the coarsely chopped walnuts and the orange zest. Pour the mixture all at once onto the prepared baking sheet; do not scrape the residue from the pan bottom. Let stand for 1 minute to firm slightly. Sprinkle the chocolate evenly over the toffee. Let stand for 1 minute to soften; then, using the back of a metal spoon, spread the chocolate over the toffee until melted. Sprinkle with the medium-fine chopped walnuts. Refrigerate, uncovered, until the candy is firm, about 2 hours.

3 Break the toffee into 2-inch pieces. Store in an airtight container in the refrigerator for up to 3 weeks.

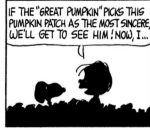

THE GREAT PUMPKIN CHEESECAKE

Lure the Great Pumpkin to your pumpkin patch with this supremely creamy and sincere cheesecake!

INGREDIENTS

FOR THE CRUST:

- 2 cups gingersnap cookie crumbs
- ¼ cup firmly packed golden brown sugar
- 5 tablespoons unsalted butter, melted and cooled

FOR THE FILLING:

- 2 lbs cream cheese, at room temperature
- 1⅓ cups firmly packed golden brown sugar
- 1⅓ cups canned pumpkin purée
- 1 tablespoon pure vanilla extract
- 1½ teaspoons ground cinnamon
- ¼ teaspoon ground allspice
- 5 large eggs, at room temperature

1 Preheat the oven to 350°F.

2 To make the crust, in a food processor fitted with a metal blade, combine the gingersnap crumbs and brown sugar. Process to mix well. Add the melted butter and process until the crumbs begin to stick together. Press the crumbs firmly onto the bottom and 2 inches up the sides of a 9-inch springform pan. Wrap aluminum foil around the outside of the pan. Bake the crust until set, about 10 minutes. Remove from the oven and set aside to cool. Leave the oven on.

3 To make the filling, in a large bowl, using an electric mixer, beat the cream cheese and brown sugar on medium speed until well blended. Beat in the pumpkin, vanilla, cinnamon, and allspice. Add the eggs one at a time, beating after each addition just until combined. Pour the filling into the cooled crust, spreading it to the edges of the pan.

4 Bake until the cheesecake puffs and the center is almost set, about 1½ hours. Transfer to a rack and let cool for 1 hour. Leave the oven on.

CONTINUED on page 72 . . .

ON HALLOWEEN NIGHT, THE "GREAT PUMPKIN" RISES OUT OF THE PUMPKIN PATCH, AND..

YOU'RE JUST TRYING TO MESS WITH MY MIND, AREN'T YOU?

. . . CONTINUED from page 70

FOR THE TOPPING:

1 cup hazelnuts

¼ cup firmly packed golden brown sugar

¼ cup unsalted butter

¼ cup heavy cream

Makes 12 servings

5 While the cheesecake is cooling, make the topping. Spread the hazelnuts on a rimmed baking sheet and bake until lightly toasted, about 10 minutes. Wrap the hazelnuts in a clean kitchen towel and let cool slightly, about 1 minute, then rub the nuts in the towel to remove the loose skins. Some specks of skin will remain.

6 In a small, heavy saucepan, combine the brown sugar, butter, and cream and cook over medium heat, stirring until the sugar dissolves. Raise the heat and bring to a boil. Add the hazelnuts and boil, stirring occasionally, until the mixture thinly coats the nuts, about 2 minutes. Spoon the topping evenly over the cooled cake and let cool. Cover with aluminum foil and refrigerate overnight or for up to 4 days.

7 To serve, run a knife around the pan sides to loosen the cake. Remove the foil from the pan and release the pan sides. Place the cheesecake on a plate and cut into wedges.

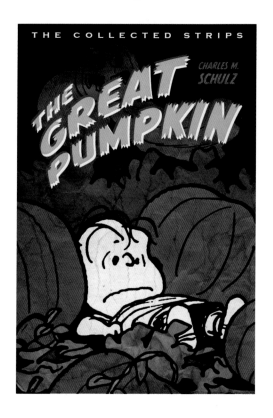

THE COLLECTED STRIPS

CHARLES M. SCHULZ

THE GREAT PUMPKIN

HERE'S THE WORLD WAR I FLYING ACE SITTING IN A LITTLE CAFE...ONCE AGAIN HE IS DEPRESSED...

HIS LEAVE IS OVER, AND HE HAS FAILED TO MEET THE CHARMING FRENCH LASS...

HE DECIDES TO FORGET HER BY DRINKING ROOT BEER...GARÇON! ANOTHER ROUND, S'IL VOUS PLAÎT!

UNFORTUNATELY, IT'S VERY HARD TO FORGET ANYONE BY DRINKING ROOT BEER!

FLYING ACE ROOT BEER FLOAT

Toast to Snoopy and service people everywhere with this delicious and fizzy Veteran's Day float.

INGREDIENTS

2 cans (12 oz each) cold
   root beer
4 scoops vanilla ice cream
Whipped cream for garnish

Makes 2 servings

1 Pour the root beer into 2 glass beer mugs, filling each one about three-fourths full.

2 Carefully drop 2 scoops of ice cream into each glass.

3 Top with whipped cream and serve.

APPLE CHARLOTTE BRAUN

A charlotte is a molded dessert with fruit filling encased in a crust of bread. You'll be shouting for more after you taste the tender apples and crisp crust in this delicious dessert!

INGREDIENTS

1¼ cups unsalted butter

6 lbs Golden Delicious apples, peeled, cored, and thinly sliced

1½ cups granulated sugar

3 teaspoons pure vanilla extract

1 loaf home-style sliced white bread

Confectioners' sugar for dusting

Whipped cream for serving

Makes 8 to 10 servings

1 Follow the instructions on page 121 to clarify 1 cup of the butter and set aside to cool.

2 In a sauté pan, melt the remaining ¼ cup butter over medium heat. Add the apples, granulated sugar, and vanilla and cook, stirring frequently, until the apples are just cooked and transparent and any juice has evaporated, 20–25 minutes. Do not let the apples burn.

3 Preheat the oven to 425°F.

4 Using a 2-inch round cutter, cut out 10 circles from the sliced bread. Dip the bread circles in the clarified butter and arrange in an overlapping pattern in the bottom of a standard 8-cup charlotte mold or 1½-qt soufflé dish. Remove the crusts from 9 slices of bread and cut each slice in half lengthwise. Dip each bread piece in the butter and vertically line the mold, overlapping the slices slightly. They should extend up to or slightly above the top of the mold. Spoon the apple slices into the mold, packing them well. Cover the surface of the apples with additional slices of crustless bread, cut to fit and dipped in clarified butter.

5 Bake the charlotte until golden brown, 30–35 minutes. Let the charlotte cool for 15 minutes. Invert the charlotte onto a serving plate and lift off the mold. Using a fine-mesh sieve, dust lightly with confectioners' sugar. Cut into slices and serve with whipped cream.

PIGPEN'S PECAN PIE

This classic pie is standard fare for Thanksgiving feasts. Your family and friends will be so pleased, they won't even mind if you make a mess!

INGREDIENTS

Flour for dusting

1 recipe Flaky Pie Dough for Single Crust (page 121), chilled

3 large eggs

½ cup sugar

1 cup dark corn syrup

1 teaspoon pure vanilla extract

¼ cup unsalted butter, melted

1½ cups pecan halves, coarsely chopped

Whipped cream for serving

Makes 6 to 8 servings

1 On a lightly floured work surface, roll out the dough into a round about 12 inches in diameter and about ⅛ inch thick. Line a 9-inch pie pan with the dough round. Trim the edges, leaving a ¾-inch overhang. Fold the overhang under itself and pinch to create a decorative edge. Refrigerate or freeze the dough until firm, about 30 minutes.

2 Preheat the oven to 400°F.

3 Line the pie shell with aluminum foil and fill with pie weights or dried beans. Bake until the crust starts to look dry, about 15 minutes. Remove the foil and weights and continue baking until lightly golden, about 5 minutes longer. Let cool completely.

4 In a large bowl, whisk together the eggs, sugar, corn syrup, and vanilla until blended, then whisk in the melted butter. Stir in the pecans. Pour the filling into the prebaked crust.

5 Bake the pie until the filling is set but the center still jiggles slightly when the pan is gently shaken, 45–50 minutes. Let cool on a wire rack. Serve warm or at room temperature, topped with whipped cream.

SNOOPY'S DOG-DISH APPLE PIE

What is Thanksgiving without apple pie? For this deep-dish version, tart baking apples are tucked inside a buttery double crust.

INGREDIENTS

1 recipe Flaky Pie Dough for Double Crust (page 121), chilled

Flour for dusting

½ cup sugar

½ teaspoon ground cinnamon

⅛ teaspoon salt

1 tablespoon cornstarch

7 large, tart, firm apples, peeled, cored, and sliced ½ inch thick

2 tablespoon cold unsalted butter, cut into small pieces

Vanilla ice cream for serving (optional)

Makes 6 to 8 servings

1 Position a rack in the lower third of the oven and preheat to 350°F.

2 Place the dough on a lightly floured work surface and cut in half. Roll each half into a round about 12 inches in diameter and about ⅛ inch thick. Line a 9-inch pie pan with one of the rounds. Trim the edges, leaving a ¾-inch overhang. Set the second dough round in a cool place until ready to use.

3 In a large bowl, stir together the sugar, cinnamon, salt, and cornstarch. Add the sliced apples and toss to coat. Dump the apples into the dough-lined pan. Dot with the butter.

4 Place the reserved dough round over the filled pie. Trim the edges, leaving a 1-inch overhang. Fold the overhang under the edge of the bottom round and crimp to seal. Using a small knife, cut 5 or 6 slits in the top of the pie.

5 Bake until the crust is golden and the apples are tender, 60–70 minutes. Let cool in the pan on a wire rack until just slightly warm, about 45 minutes. If you like, top each serving with ice cream.

LINUS'S MARSHMALLOW HOT CHOCOLATE

Ah, the sweet taste of hot chocolate topped with marshmallows . . . made even sweeter when served by a little brother at Christmas.

INGREDIENTS

⅓ cup unsweetened cocoa powder

¼ cup sugar

Pinch of salt

3 cups milk

½ teaspoon pure vanilla extract

9 large marshmallows, store-bought or homemade (see page 44)

Makes 4 servings

1 Combine the cocoa, sugar, and salt in a saucepan and stir with a wooden spoon until well blended. Add a small amount of the milk and stir to make a smooth paste, then stir in the remaining milk.

2 Cook the mixture over medium heat, stirring constantly, until tiny bubbles form around the edges of the pan, about 8 minutes. Do not boil.

3 Reduce the heat to low. Add the vanilla and 5 of the marshmallows. Cook, stirring constantly, until the marshmallows melt, about 5 minutes.

4 Ladle the hot chocolate into 4 mugs. Add 1 marshmallow to each mug and serve immediately.

PEPPERMINT PATTYPUCKS

If thin mints are one of your favorite cookies, then you'll love these minty, chocolate–dipped wafers . . . perfect for Christmas parties or hockey practice!

INGREDIENTS

FOR THE COOKIES:

1¼ cups all-purpose flour, plus flour as needed

¾ cup sugar

¾ cup unsweetened Dutch-process cocoa powder

1 teaspoon baking soda

¼ teaspoon baking powder

½ teaspoon salt

¾ cup unsalted butter, at room temperature

1 large egg

1 teaspoon pure vanilla extract

½ teaspoon peppermint extract

1 tablespoon heavy cream

1 To make the cookies, whisk together the flour, sugar, cocoa powder, baking soda, baking powder, and salt in a medium bowl. In a large bowl, using an electric mixer, beat the butter on medium speed until light and fluffy, about 3 minutes. Add the egg and beat on low speed until well blended. Add the flour mixture and beat on low speed until combined, about 2 minutes. Turn off the mixer and scrape down the bowl with a silicone spatula. Add the vanilla and peppermint extracts and the cream. Raise the speed to medium and beat until the dough comes together, about 2 minutes.

2 Scrape the dough onto a work surface. Using your hands, form the dough into a disk, wrap it tightly in plastic wrap, and refrigerate until well chilled, about 30 minutes.

3 Preheat the oven to 375°F. Line 2 baking sheets with parchment paper.

4 On a floured work surface, roll out the dough until about ¼-inch thick. Using a 2½-inch round cookie cutter, cut out rounds from the dough. Using a metal spatula, carefully move the cutouts to the prepared baking sheets, spacing them about 1 inch apart. Gather the dough scraps and press them together, then roll them out and cut out more rounds. If the dough is too soft and sticky to roll, wrap it in plastic wrap and refrigerate until slightly firm, about 15 minutes.

CONTINUED on page 84 . . .

. . . CONTINUED from page 83

FOR THE GLAZE:

1 ¼ lb semisweet or
  bittersweet chocolate,
  finely chopped
½ teaspoon canola oil
½ teaspoon peppermint
  extract

Makes about 40 cookies

5 Bake 1 baking sheet at a time until the centers of the cookies are firm to the touch, 8–10 minutes. (Be careful when touching the cookies—they're very hot!) Set the sheet on a wire rack to cool for 5 minutes, then transfer the cookies to the rack and let cool completely. Repeat to bake the remaining cookies. Let cool completely. Reserve the parchment-lined baking sheets.

6 To make the glaze, place the chocolate in a medium microwave-safe bowl. Microwave on high power, stirring after 30 seconds, then after every 15 seconds, just until melted and smooth. Don't let it get too hot! Stir in the oil and peppermint extract.

7 Dip each cookie into the glaze and use 2 forks to turn the cookie so that it's coated on both sides. Using the forks, lift out the cookie and gently shake it, allowing excess glaze to fall back into the bowl. Place the glazed cookie back on 1 of the parchment-lined baking sheets. Repeat with the remaining cookies and glaze. (If the glaze starts to harden, microwave it on high power, stirring every 15 seconds, until it has remelted.)

8 Refrigerate the cookies uncovered until the glaze is set, about 20 minutes. Serve the cookies chilled or at room temperature. To store the cookies, layer them between pieces of parchment paper in an airtight container. They will keep for up to 3 days in the refrigerator.

THE GOOSE EGGS' NOG

This eggnog, topped with sweetened whipped cream and freshly ground spices, is a kid-friendly version of the traditional Christmas drink.

INGREDIENTS

12 large egg yolks

4 cups whole milk

1¼ cups sugar

2 cups heavy cream

½ teaspoon pure vanilla extract

1 teaspoon nutmeg

1 teaspoon cinnamon

Makes 8 to 10 servings

1 In a large saucepan, whisk together the egg yolks, 2 cups of the milk, and 1 cup of the sugar. Simmer over low heat, stirring often, until slightly thickened, 8–10 minutes. Remove from the heat, stir in the remaining 2 cups milk, and let cool.

2 Strain the cooled egg mixture through a fine-mesh sieve into a serving pitcher or a punch bowl. Refrigerate until thoroughly chilled, at least 3 hours or up to overnight.

3 In a bowl, using a handheld mixer or whisk, whip the cream with the remaining ¼ cup sugar and the vanilla until soft peaks form. Serve the eggnog in cups or glasses, topped with a dollop of the sweetened whipped cream and a sprinkle each of nutmeg and cinnamon.

QUICK, MARCIE, WHAT'S THE ANSWER TO THE FIRST QUESTION?

I CAN'T TELL YOU, SIR..THAT WOULD BE CHEATING..

YOU'RE RIGHT, MARCIE..WHAT WAS I THINKING?

WHAT CAME OVER ME? IT'S SO UNLIKE ME! I MUST HAVE BLANKED OUT!

TEN!

GOT IT!

MARCIE'S NO-FUDGE FUDGE

This rich fudge, which is lightened by a smattering of airy marshmallows, is so good, you might do anything for a second helping!

INGREDIENTS

$^1/_2$ cup unsalted butter, melted

2 cups firmly packed golden brown sugar

2 cups granulated sugar

1 cup half-and-half

$^1/_2$ cup light corn syrup

$^1/_4$ teaspoon salt

8 oz bittersweet or semisweet chocolate, coarsely chopped

2 cups miniature marshmallows

Makes about 32 squares

1 Lightly grease a 9 × 11-inch or 9 × 13-inch baking pan.

2 In a large, heavy saucepan, bring the butter, both sugars, half-and-half, corn syrup, and salt to a boil over medium heat, stirring constantly. Using a pastry brush dipped in hot water, brush down any sugar crystals that form on the sides of the pan. Boil for 2½ minutes, then add the chocolate and stir until melted and well blended. Continue to boil, without stirring, until a candy thermometer clipped to the side of the pan reads 234°F, 7–10 minutes.

3 Remove from the heat and let cool until almost room temperature, or 110°F on the thermometer, about 15 minutes. Using an electric mixer, beat the fudge until the color dulls and the fudge is creamy, 2–3 minutes.

4 Scatter half of the marshmallows in the prepared pan and spoon half of the fudge over them. Scatter the remaining marshmallows on top, then spoon over the remaining fudge. Smooth the surface of the fudge with a silicone spatula, pressing the marshmallows and fudge together. Cover the pan with aluminum foil and refrigerate until firm, about 6 hours. Cut into squares and serve. Wrap leftovers tightly in aluminum foil and store in the refrigerator for up to 1 week.

VARIATION: For a rocky road variation, add 1 cup chopped toasted almonds with the marshmallows.

SNOOPY'S GINGERBREAD DOGHOUSE

There's nothing like the aroma of gingerbread to get you in the holiday spirit. Spread your good cheer by making and decorating a doghouse for Snoopy!

INGREDIENTS

FOR THE DOUGH:

8 cups all-purpose flour, plus flour for dusting

2 teaspoons ground ginger

1½ teaspoons ground cinnamon

1 teaspoon ground cloves

2¼ cups solid vegetable shortening

2 cups granulated sugar

2 large eggs

1 cup light (unsulfured) molasses

⅔ cup light corn syrup

1 To make a gingerbread doghouse, you will first need to make a template for cutting the dough. Download a doghouse template from the Internet or make your own, drawing a front and back of the house (each one a 5-inch square topped with a triangle for the peaked roof), two sides (5 inches high × 6 inches wide), and two roof panels (6 inches wide × 7 inches long). When ready to construct and decorate the house, draw a 6 × 5-inch rectangle (or the size of the house perimeter of your downloaded template) on a piece of parchment paper and place it on a flat platter or tray.

2 Preheat the oven to 350°F. Line 2 rimmed baking sheets with parchment paper.

3 To make the dough, in a large mixing bowl, combine the flour, ginger, cinnamon, and cloves. In another large bowl, using an electric mixer, beat the shortening and granulated sugar on medium speed till fluffy. Add the eggs, molasses, and corn syrup and beat until combined. Add the flour mixture gradually and beat well. If necessary, stir in the last 2 cups of the flour mixture by hand and knead the dough until smooth.

CONTINUED on page 90 . . .

PEANUTS

Panel 1: I WORRY ABOUT THIS TIME OF YEAR..

Panel 2: I REMEMBER LAST YEAR ABOUT THIS TIME...IT WAS TWO O'CLOCK IN THE MORNING, AND I WAS SOUND ASLEEP...

Panel 3: SUDDENLY, OUT OF NOWHERE, THIS CRAZY GUY WITH A SLED LANDS RIGHT ON MY ROOF

Panel 4: HE WAS OKAY, BUT THOSE STUPID REINDEER KEPT STEPPING ON MY STOMACH!

. . . CONTINUED from page 89

FOR THE ICING:

3 large egg whites, at room
   temperature

1 lb confectioners' sugar,
   sifted

1 teaspoon pure vanilla
   extract

½ teaspoon cream of tartar

FOR DECORATION:

Assortment of red and green
   gumdrops

12 round peppermint candies

Confectioners' sugar for
   dusting (optional)

Makes 1 gingerbread
doghouse

4 Divide the dough in half. On a lightly floured surface, using a floured rolling pin, roll out 1 dough piece until about ⅜ inch thick. Cover the dough with one each of the house patterns for a front or back wall, side wall, and roof panel (see step 1). Using the tip of a sharp knife or a pizza cutter, cut out the dough pieces using the patterns as a guide, then transfer the pieces to one of the prepared baking sheets. Repeat with the remaining dough, placing the dough pieces on the second prepared baking sheet. Cut a dog door into the front panel. Set aside any remaining dough to use in another recipe.

5 Bake the dough panels, switching the pans halfway through baking, until the edges are lightly browned, 10–12 minutes. Set the sheet on a wire rack to cool for 5 minutes, then transfer the cookies to the rack and let cool completely. (If you allow the pieces to dry overnight, they will be even firmer and better for construction.)

6 To make the icing, in a large bowl, using an electric mixer, beat the egg whites, confectioners' sugar, vanilla, and cream of tartar on high speed until stiff peaks form, 7–10 minutes. Cover the icing with plastic wrap to prevent drying. Fill a lock-top plastic bag with about ½ cup of the icing mixture, press out the air, and seal. Snip off a corner.

7 Pipe a line of icing on the perimeter of the parchment template. Set the bottoms of the front and back panels and the side panels into the icing on the template to make the 4 walls of the house. Pipe a line of icing along the edge of the panels at the 4 corners of the house and hold the panels together until stable; if needed, prop them up with heavy cans of food. Pipe a line of the remaining icing along the top edge of each panel, then set the roof pieces on top. (You might need someone to help you hold all the pieces together.) Pipe a line along the top peak of the house to help secure the roof panels and cover any holes. Let stand until set, about 1 hour.

8 Using the icing as glue and snow, decorate the gingerbread house, adhering the gumdrops and peppermint candies to the house as desired.

9 Let stand until set, about 1 hour. Dust with confectioners' sugar, if desired, to mimic snow.

KITE—EATING TREE BARK

Chewy dried cherries and crunchy toasted almonds stud bittersweet chocolate, making this yummy Christmas bark definitely worth the bite!

INGREDIENTS

7 oz bittersweet or semisweet chocolate, chopped

1 oz unsweetened chocolate, chopped

³/₄ cup chopped whole almonds, toasted

³/₄ cup dried sour cherries

Makes about 12 oz

1 Grease a rimmed baking sheet and line with parchment paper.

2 Combine the chocolates in a heatproof bowl set over but not touching simmering water in a saucepan and heat, stirring occasionally, until melted and smooth.

3 Stir ½ cup of the almonds and ½ cup of the cherries into the melted chocolate, then pour the mixture onto the prepared baking sheet, tilting to spread slightly. Scatter the remaining ¼ cup each almonds and cherries evenly over the top. Refrigerate the candy, uncovered, until firm, about 1 hour.

4 Gently peel the candy from the parchment paper. Then, holding the candy with the parchment (to prevent fingerprints), break the chocolate into large, irregular pieces. Store in an airtight container at cool room temperature for up to 5 days.

FRANKLIN'S FRUITCAKE

This cake, which calls for dried fruits instead of candied fruits, is so tasty everyone will want some. Choose a mixture of any nuts you like!

INGREDIENTS

1 cup chopped dried pears

1 cup chopped dried apricots

1 cup chopped pitted prunes

½ cup chopped pitted dates

½ cup dark raisins

½ cup golden raisins

3 tablespoons finely chopped candied orange peel

2 tablespoons finely chopped crystallized ginger

½ cup water

1 tablespoon pure vanilla extract

1½ cups unsalted butter, at room temperature

2½ cups sugar

8 large eggs, at room temperature

3 cups sifted cake flour

½ teaspoon salt

2 cups chopped nuts, toasted

Makes 16 to 18 servings

1 Preheat the oven to 325°F. Grease a 10-inch tube pan. Line the bottom with parchment paper cut to fit exactly. Grease the paper, then flour the paper and pan sides.

2 In a bowl, combine the pears, apricots, prunes, dates, dark and golden raisins, orange peel, and ginger. In a cup, mix the water and vanilla and pour over the top. Let stand for at least 4 hours or as long as overnight at room temperature, stirring occasionally.

3 In a large bowl, using an electric mixer, beat the butter on medium speed until light and fluffy, about 7 minutes. Add the sugar and beat until once again fluffy, about 4 minutes. Add the eggs one at a time, beating well after each addition. Reduce the speed to low and beat in the flour and salt. Using a wooden spoon, fold in the nuts and fruit until fully incorporated.

4 Spoon the batter into the prepared pan. Using the back of a wooden spoon, spread the batter evenly and smooth the top. Bake until a toothpick inserted near the center of the cake comes out clean, about 1 hour 50 minutes. Transfer to a rack and let cool in the pan for 5 minutes. Invert the cake onto the rack, then carefully lift off the pan and peel off the paper. Let cool completely before serving.

SNOOPY'S SNOWFLAKES

Crisp and full of flavor, these snowflake-shaped gingersnaps will be the start of a delicious new holiday tradition. Let it snow!

INGREDIENTS

6 cups all-purpose flour, plus flour as needed

1 tablespoon baking soda

1 cup unsalted butter, at room temperature

2½ cups granulated sugar

¾ cup dark corn syrup

¾ cup water

1 tablespoon ground cinnamon

1 tablespoon ground cloves

1 tablespoon ground ginger

1 recipe Vanilla Icing (page 119)

White sanding sugar, for decorating (optional)

Makes about 48 cookies

1 In a large bowl, whisk together the flour and baking soda. In another large bowl, using an electric mixer, beat the butter and granulated sugar on medium speed until light and fluffy, about 3 minutes. Set aside.

2 In a medium saucepan, combine the corn syrup, water, and spices. Bring the mixture to a boil over medium-high heat, stirring occasionally. Turn off the heat and let cool for 5 minutes. Pour the corn syrup mixture into the butter-sugar mixture and stir until combined. Gradually stir in the flour mixture, mixing just until combined. Using floured hands, form the dough into a rectangle, wrap it tightly in plastic wrap, and refrigerate until firm, about 2 hours.

3 Preheat the oven to 350°F. Line 2 baking sheets with parchment paper.

4 Cut the dough into 4 pieces. On a floured work surface, roll out 1 piece of dough until about ¼-inch thick. Using snowflake cookie cutters, cut out shapes from the dough. Transfer the cutouts to the prepared baking sheets, spacing them about 1 inch apart. Repeat with the remaining pieces of dough. Gather the dough scraps and press them together, then roll them out and cut out more snowflakes.

5 Bake 1 baking sheet at a time until the cookies are firm to the touch, 10–12 minutes. Set the sheet on a wire rack to cool for 5 minutes, then transfer the cookies to the rack and let cool completely. Repeat to bake the remaining cookies.

6 Decorate the cookies with vanilla icing and sanding sugar as desired. Let the icing dry at room temperature until firm, at least 2 hours or up to overnight.

YULE (REGRET IT) LOG

You won't regret making this classic Christmas cake, inspired by the yule log.

INGREDIENTS

1 cup all-purpose flour

$3/4$ teaspoon baking powder

$1/4$ teaspoon salt

4 large eggs

$2/3$ cup granulated sugar

$1^{1}/4$ teaspoons pure vanilla
extract

Confectioners' sugar for
dusting

Chocolate Fudge Frosting
(see page 120)

Makes 10 to 12 servings

1 Preheat the oven to 350°F. Grease a 10 x 15-inch rimmed baking sheet and line the bottom with parchment paper. Grease the paper and the pan sides and dust with flour.

2 To make the cake, sift the flour, baking powder, and salt into a bowl. In a large bowl, using an electric mixer, beat the eggs on medium-high speed until pale and thick, about 3 minutes. Add the granulated sugar and vanilla and continue beating until tripled in volume, about 3 minutes.

3 Sprinkle the dry ingredients over the egg mixture and, using a silicone spatula, fold gently just until blended. Pour the batter into the prepared pan and spread evenly. Bake until the cake springs back when lightly touched, 13–15 minutes.

4 Lay a kitchen towel on a work surface and sift confectioners' sugar generously onto it, covering it evenly. Remove the cake from the oven and run a knife around the inside of the pan to loosen the cake. Holding the cake in place, invert the pan onto the prepared towel. Lift off the pan and carefully peel off the paper. Beginning on a long edge, roll up the cake and towel together. Set on a rack and let cool.

5 Unroll the cake. Spread a third of the frosting over the cake. Gently reroll the cake (without the towel) and place, seam side down, on a cutting board. Spread the remaining frosting on the top and sides of the roll, then run the knife tip down the length of the cake to simulate bark. Using a serrated knife, trim each end at a sharp angle. Transfer the cake to a plate and serve.

SPARKLING CANDY CANE COOKIES

These bedazzling and delightful twisted confections sparkle with shimmery sweetness.

INGREDIENTS

2¹/₂ cups all-purpose flour, plus more for dusting

1 teaspoon baking powder

¹/₂ teaspoon salt

1 cup unsalted butter, at room temperature

³/₄ cup granulated sugar

3 large egg yolks

1¹/₂ teaspoons pure vanilla extract

Red food coloring

1 egg white

1 tablespoon white sparkling sugar

Makes about 24 cookies

1 In a bowl, sift together the flour, baking powder, and salt. Set aside. In the bowl of a stand mixer fitted with the paddle attachment, beat the butter and granulated sugar on medium speed until light and fluffy, about 3 minutes. Reduce the speed to low and add the egg yolks one at a time, beating well after each addition. Add the vanilla and beat until combined, about 1 minute. Stop the mixer and scrape down the sides of the bowl. Add the flour mixture and beat on low speed until combined, about 1 minute.

2 Turn out the dough onto a work surface, divide into 2 equal pieces. Put 1 piece in the bowl of a stand mixer fitted with the paddle attachment and add a few drops of the red food coloring. Mix on medium-low speed until completely combined. Shape each piece into a disk, wrap separately in plastic wrap, and refrigerate overnight. Let the dough soften slightly at room temperature before continuing.

3 Preheat the oven to 350°F. Line a rimmed baking sheet with parchment paper.

4 On a floured work surface, roll out the red dough disk ¼ inch thick. Cut the dough into strips 6 inches long and ¾ inch wide. Repeat with the plain dough. (Alternatively, you can roll each dough disk into a long rope about ¾ inch thick and cut the ropes into 6-inch lengths.) Taking 1 red strip and 1 plain strip, pinch the ends together and gently twist the strips around each other. Pinch the other end to secure and bend one end into a hook to form a candy cane shape.

5 Transfer to the prepared baking sheet. In a small bowl, lightly beat the egg white. Brush the egg white over the cookie twists, then sprinkle evenly with the sparkling sugar. Repeat with the remaining dough, spacing the cookies about 1½ inches apart. Bake until the cookies are golden on the edges, about 8 minutes. Set the sheet on a wire rack to cool for 5 minutes, then transfer the cookies to the rack and let cool completely.

SLINGSHOT SNOWBALLS

These traditional northern European "pepper nut" cookies, *pfeffernuesse*, look like little sugary snowballs. Just make sure to aim for your mouth!

INGREDIENTS

2¼ cups all-purpose flour

½ teaspoon salt

½ teaspoon ground black pepper

½ teaspoon crushed aniseed

½ teaspoon ground cinnamon

¼ teaspoon baking soda

¼ teaspoon ground allspice

¼ teaspoon ground nutmeg

⅛ teaspoon ground cloves

½ cup unsalted butter, at room temperature

¾ cup firmly packed golden brown sugar

¼ cup light (unsulfured) molasses

1 large egg

2 cups confectioners' sugar

Makes about 30 cookies

1 In a medium bowl, sift together the flour, salt, pepper, aniseed, cinnamon, baking soda, allspice, nutmeg, and cloves. In a large bowl, using an electric mixer, beat the butter, brown sugar, and molasses on medium speed until light and fluffy, about 4 minutes. Beat in the egg. Reduce the mixer speed to low and beat in the flour mixture. Cover and refrigerate for several hours.

2 Preheat the oven to 350°F. Grease 2 rimmed baking sheets.

3 Scoop up pieces of the dough and roll between your palms into balls 1½ inches in diameter. Place the balls on the baking sheets, spacing them about 2 inches apart.

4 Bake until the cookies are golden brown on the bottom and firm to the touch, about 14 minutes. Transfer the baking sheets to racks and let the cookies cool slightly on the sheets. Put the confectioners' sugar in a sturdy paper bag. Drop a few warm cookies into the bag, close the top securely, and shake gently to coat the cookies with the sugar. Transfer to the racks. Repeat with the remaining cookies. Let cool completely before serving.

5 Store in an airtight container at cool room temperature for up to 1 week.

NO–BAKE COCONUT CANDIES

You'll love the sweet crunch of chocolate, coconut, and macadamia nuts in these delectable Christmas treats. And there's no need to turn on the oven!

INGREDIENTS

10 oz milk chocolate, chopped

3 oz bittersweet or semisweet chocolate, chopped

2 cups coarsely chopped lightly salted roasted macadamia nuts

1 cup sweetened shredded coconut, lightly toasted (see Note)

Makes 48 candies

1 Line a rimmed baking sheet with parchment paper.

2 Combine the chocolates in a heatproof bowl set over but not touching simmering water in a saucepan. Heat the chocolate, stirring constantly, until it is melted and smooth. Pour off the hot water from the saucepan and replace it with lukewarm water. Replace the bowl. Let the chocolate stand, stirring frequently, until it cools slightly and begins to thicken, about 10 minutes.

3 Stir the macadamia nuts and toasted coconut into the chocolate, mixing thoroughly. Using a small spoon, scoop out slightly rounded teaspoons of the mixture and drop onto the prepared sheet, spacing them evenly. Refrigerate, uncovered, until set, about 2 hours.

4 Store in an airtight container in the refrigerator for up to 1 month or in the freezer for up to 2 months.

NOTE: To toast the shredded coconut, spread evenly on a baking sheet and bake in a 350°F oven, stirring occasionally, until pale gold, about 8 minutes.

LUCY'S WUMP DUMP CAKE

Annual holiday football parties just got easier! With this recipe, you simply dump all the ingredients in the pan and bake.

INGREDIENTS

1 bag (16-oz) frozen mixed berries, slightly thawed

2 tablespoons all-purpose flour

1 (15.25-oz) package yellow cake mix

½ cup butter, thinly sliced

Vanilla ice cream for serving

Makes 12 servings

1 Preheat the oven to 350°F.

2 Mix the berries with the flour and pour into a 9 x 13-inch baking dish. Sprinkle the cake mix over the berries and stir until just combined. Arrange the butter slices in an even layer over the cake mixture.

3 Bake until golden and bubbly, about 45–50 minutes.

4 Top with ice cream and serve warm.

TRUFFLES'S TRUFFLES

This recipe uses just four ingredients, but the results are rich mounds of chocolaty goodness. Perfect for New Year's Eve!

INGREDIENTS

8 oz bittersweet or semisweet chocolate, chopped

½ cup unsalted butter, clarified (see page 121)

¾ cup heavy cream

½ cup unsweetened Dutch-process cocoa powder

Makes about 50 truffles

1 In a heatproof bowl set over but not touching simmering water in a saucepan, heat the chocolate, stirring occasionally, until melted and smooth. Remove the bowl and add the clarified butter. Stir until blended. Stir in the cream. Cover and place in the refrigerator to thicken, 10–15 minutes.

2 Spread the cocoa powder in a shallow dish. Using a teaspoon, scoop up a rounded spoonful of the thickened chocolate mixture and, with the aid of a second teaspoon, shape into a ¾-inch ball. Drop the ball into the cocoa powder and turn to coat well, then transfer to a plate. Repeat until all the chocolate has been used, then refrigerate to harden for 30–40 minutes. Roll the hardened balls in the cocoa again until completely covered. Place in a storage container.

3 Pour any remaining cocoa over the truffles and shake the container to distribute the cocoa evenly. Cover and store in the refrigerator for up to 1 week. Remove from the refrigerator about 10 minutes before serving.

CHARLIE BROWN'S TUXEDO COOKIES

Dark chocolate and snow-white glazes dress up ordinary sugar cookies—serve these gussied-up treats as you ring in the New Year!

INGREDIENTS

1 recipe Lucky Shamrock
  Cookies (no Shamrock
  Icing), page 15

FOR THE CHOCOLATE GLAZE:

¼ cup heavy cream

¼ cup unsalted butter, cut
  into ½-inch pieces

3 tablespoons light corn syrup

5 oz semisweet chocolate,
  chopped

FOR THE SNOW-WHITE GLAZE:

3 cups confectioners' sugar

¼ cup hot water

2 tablespoons light corn syrup

½ teaspoon almond extract

Makes 40 cookies

1 Follow the recipe to make and roll out the dough for the Shamrock Cookies, then cut the dough into rounds using a 3-inch round cookie cutter. Bake and cool the cookies as directed.

2 While the cookies are cooling, make the glazes. For the chocolate glaze, combine the cream, butter, corn syrup, and chocolate in a heatproof bowl set over but not touching simmering water in a saucepan. Heat, stirring constantly, until the chocolate is melted and smooth, 3–4 minutes. Set aside to cool and thicken, about 45 minutes at room temperature or 15 minutes if covered and refrigerated.

3 For the snow-white glaze, sift the confectioners' sugar into a bowl. Add the hot water, corn syrup, and almond extract and stir until smooth.

4 Line a rimmed baking sheet with waxed paper. Spoon a teaspoon of the white glaze onto each cookie. Use the back of a spoon to spread the glaze over half of the cookie. (If the glaze becomes too thick to spread, stir in a few drops of hot water.) Next, spoon 1 teaspoon of the chocolate glaze over the unglazed half of each cookie, spreading it evenly. Transfer the cookies to the prepared baking sheet and refrigerate until the glaze is firm, about 30 minutes, or cover with plastic wrap and refrigerate for up to 3 days. Bring the cookies to room temperature before serving.

SALLY'S CHOCOLATE SMACKS

Who can resist a kiss of luxurious chocolate mixed with sweet raspberries on Valentine's Day?

INGREDIENTS

4 oz semisweet chocolate, finely chopped

1½ pints raspberries

Makes about 36 candies

1 Grease a large rimmed baking sheet and line with waxed paper.

2 Put the chocolate in a heatproof bowl and place it over but not touching very hot tap water in a saucepan. Let stand, without stirring, until it begins to melt, then stir until melted and smooth.

3 Using a small spoon, drop the melted chocolate onto the waxed paper, forming rounds ¼ inch in diameter. Immediately top each round with a raspberry, rounded side up. Refrigerate, uncovered, just until the chocolate feels firm, cold, and dry, about 15 minutes.

4 Gently peel the candies from the waxed paper. Serve right away or store in an airtight container in the refrigerator for up to 2 days.

VIOLET'S VALENTINE'S CANDIES

Roll out a sweet batch of these old-fashioned butter mints and everyone will want to be your Valentine!

INGREDIENTS

2½ cups sifted confectioners' sugar, plus confectioners' sugar as needed

2 tablespoons unsalted butter, at room temperature

1½ tablespoons warm water, plus water as needed

½ teaspoon peppermint extract, plus peppermint extract as needed

Red food coloring

Makes about 50 mints

1 In a bowl, combine 1 cup of the sifted sugar, the butter, and 1 tablespoon of the warm water. Using an electric mixer, beat the mixture on medium speed until smooth. Slowly add the remaining 1½ cups sugar and ½ tablespoon water, continuing to beat until the mixture is smooth and well blended. The mixture should be soft and not sticky. If it is crumbly, add a few drops of water. If it is sticky, add a little more sugar.

2 Add the peppermint extract and use your hands to squeeze and press it into the mixture. Taste; if you want a stronger peppermint flavor, knead in a few more drops of peppermint extract.

3 Transfer half of the mixture to another bowl. Add 1–2 drops of red food coloring to one bowl and knead it in until the dough is evenly pink. Add 3–4 drops of red food coloring to the other bowl and knead until evenly red.

4 Line a baking sheet with waxed paper. Lay out 2 large sheets of waxed paper and lightly dust them with confectioners' sugar. Place the pink sugar mixture on 1 sheet of waxed paper and cover it with the other sheet of waxed paper, with the sugar-dusted side down. With the rolling pin, roll out the mixture until about ⅛ inch thick. Peel off the top sheet of paper. Use a small heart-shaped cutter to cut out the mints. Carefully transfer the cut-out mints to the lined baking sheet. Dust the waxed paper sheets again with confectioners' sugar and repeat the rolling and cutting with the red mixture. Set aside the mints until firm, about 1 hour.

5 Store the mints in an airtight container in a cool place for up to 3 days.

"LITTLE RED-HAIRED GIRL" VELVET CUPCAKES

These cupcakes are yummy enough to entice even the Little Red-Haired Girl.

INGREDIENTS

2 tablespoons unsweetened cocoa
  powder, sifted

1/3 cup boiling water

1 cup buttermilk

1 cup freeze-dried strawberries

2 cups all-purpose flour

1/4 teaspoon salt

3/4 cup unsalted butter, at room
  temperature

1 1/2 cups sugar

3 large eggs

2 teaspoons pure vanilla extract

Pink food coloring

1 1/2 teaspoons baking soda

1 teaspoon white vinegar

Strawberry–Cream Cheese
  Frosting (page 118)

Red and pink regular or
  heart-shaped sprinkles for
  decorating (optional)

Makes 20 cupcakes

1 Preheat the oven to 350°F. Line 20 cups of 2 standard 12-cup muffin pans with paper or foil liners.

2 In a heatproof bowl, whisk together the cocoa and boiling water until well combined, then whisk in the buttermilk. Set aside.

3 Put the dried strawberries in a quart-size lock-top plastic bag, press out the air, and seal the bag. Using a rolling pin or wooden spoon, crush the strawberries to a fine powder. Transfer the strawberry powder to a small bowl and whisk in the flour and salt.

4 In a large bowl, using an electric mixer, beat the butter and sugar on medium speed until light and fluffy, 2–3 minutes. Add the eggs one at a time, beating well after each addition. Add the vanilla and 3 drops of food coloring and beat until combined. Add half of the flour mixture and mix on low speed just until blended. Pour in the cocoa mixture and mix on low speed until combined. Add the remaining flour mixture and beat just until blended. In a small bowl, stir together the baking soda and vinegar, then quickly add the mixture to the batter and stir with a silicone spatula until combined.

5 Divide the batter evenly among the prepared muffin cups. Bake until a toothpick inserted into the center of a cupcake comes out clean, about 18 minutes. Set the pans on a wire rack and let cool for 10 minutes, then transfer the cupcakes to the rack and let cool completely, about 1 hour.

6 Using a pastry bag fitted with a star tip, frost the cupcakes with the Strawberry–Cream Cheese Frosting, then decorate them with sprinkles, if desired.

BASIC RECIPES

STRAWBERRY– CREAM CHEESE FROSTING

INGREDIENTS

2 packages (8 oz each) cream cheese, at room temperature

12 tablespoons unsalted butter, at room temperature

2 teaspoons pure vanilla extract

2 cups confectioners' sugar

1 cup freeze-dried strawberries

Makes about 3 cups

In a large bowl, using an electric mixer, beat the cream cheese, butter, and vanilla on medium-high speed until light and fluffy, about 2 minutes. Turn off the mixer and scrape down the bowl with a silicone spatula. Add about half of the confectioners' sugar and mix on low speed until well blended. Turn off the mixer, add the remaining sugar, and beat on medium speed until smooth. The frosting should be spreadable; if it is too soft, cover the bowl and refrigerate for about 15 minutes.

Put the freeze-dried strawberries in a quart-size lock-top plastic bag, press out the air, and seal the bag. Using a rolling pin or wooden spoon, crush the strawberries to a fine powder. Add the strawberry powder to the cream cheese frosting and mix on low speed until well combined. Use right away.

VANILLA ICING

INGREDIENTS

2 cups confectioners' sugar

2 tablespoons warm water, plus water as needed

1 tablespoon light corn syrup

1 teaspoon pure vanilla extract

Makes about ½ cup

In a medium bowl, whisk together the confectioners' sugar, water, corn syrup, and vanilla until smooth. Add more water if the icing is too thick. Use right away.

SHAMROCK ICING: Make the icing as directed, stirring in 5–6 drops green food coloring with the vanilla.

LEMON ICING

INGREDIENTS

¼ cup unsalted butter

½ teaspoon grated lemon zest

1 tablespoon lemon juice

½ cup confectioners' sugar

Makes about ½ cup

In a small saucepan, combine the butter, lemon zest, and lemon juice and heat over medium heat until the butter melts. Remove from the heat and let stand until cool, about 5 minutes. Add the sugar and whisk vigorously until smooth and thickened, about 1 minute. Use right away.

CREAM CHEESE FROSTING

INGREDIENTS

4 oz cream cheese, at room temperature

6 tablespoons unsalted butter, at room temperature

1 teaspoon pure vanilla extract

2 cups confectioners' sugar

Makes about 1½ cups

In a large bowl, using a handheld mixer or a stand mixer fitted with the paddle attachment, beat together the cream cheese, butter, and vanilla on medium speed until smooth, about 2 minutes. Stop the mixer and scrape down the sides of the bowl with a silicone spatula. With the mixer on low speed, gradually beat in half of the sugar until incorporated. Turn off the mixer, add the remaining sugar, and beat on medium speed until smooth. Use right away.

CHOCOLATE FUDGE FROSTING

INGREDIENTS

¼ cup unsalted butter

¼ cup heavy cream

2 cups semisweet or bittersweet chocolate, coarsely chopped

¾ cup sour cream

1¼ cups confectioners' sugar

Makes about 2²/₃ CUPS

In a heavy saucepan, combine the butter and cream and heat over low heat, stirring often, until the butter melts. Add the chocolate and stir until melted and smooth, about 2 minutes. Remove from the heat and let cool to lukewarm.

Whisk in the sour cream until fully combined. Sift the confectioners' sugar over the chocolate, whisking constantly until no lumps remain. Let the frosting cool and thicken, whisking every 10 minutes, until thick enough to spread, about 30 minutes. Use right away.

VANILLA FROSTING

INGREDIENTS

¾ cup unsalted butter, at room temperature

3¼ cups confectioners' sugar

2 tablespoons heavy cream

2 teaspoons pure vanilla extract

¼ teaspoon salt

Makes about 2¼ cups

In a bowl, using an electric mixer, beat the butter, sugar, cream, vanilla, and salt on low speed until creamy and smooth, about 3 minutes. Use right away.

PRETZEL TREES

INGREDIENTS

12 pretzel sticks

½ cup green candy melts or semisweet chocolate chips

Makes 12 trees

Line a small baking sheet with parchment paper. Arrange the pretzel sticks about 3 inches apart on the parchment paper. Put the candy melts in a small bowl. Microwave on high power, stirring after 30 seconds, then after every 15 seconds, just until melted and smooth. Spoon the melted candy into a small piping bag with a plain tip or a small plastic bag with a corner snipped. Using a short sweeping motion, drizzle the melted candy over one end of each pretzel to resemble the branches of a tree. Refrigerate until set, about 10 minutes. Carefully remove the trees from the parchment.

FLAKY PIE DOUGH FOR SINGLE CRUST

INGREDIENTS
1¼ cups all-purpose flour
¼ teaspoon salt
2 teaspoons sugar
7 tablespoons cold unsalted butter, cut into pieces
5 tablespoons ice water, plus more if needed

Makes one 9-inch pie crust

In the bowl of a food processor, combine the flour, salt, and sugar. Sprinkle the butter over the top and pulse for a few seconds, or just until the butter is slightly broken up into the flour but still in visible pieces. Evenly sprinkle the water over the flour mixture, then process just until the mixture starts to come together. Dump the dough into a large lock-top plastic bag and press into a flat disk. Refrigerate for at least 30 minutes and up to 1 day before using, or freeze for up to 1 month.

FLAKY PIE DOUGH FOR DOUBLE CRUST

INGREDIENTS
2 cups all-purpose flour
½ teaspoon salt
1 tablespoon sugar
¾ cup cold unsalted butter, cut into pieces
½ cup ice water, plus more if needed

Makes two 9-inch pie crusts

In the bowl of a food processor, combine the flour, salt, and sugar. Sprinkle the butter over the top and pulse for a few seconds, or just until the butter is slightly broken up into the flour but still in visible pieces. Evenly sprinkle the water over the flour mixture, then process just until the mixture starts to come together. Dump the dough into a large lock-top plastic bag and press into a flat disk. Refrigerate for at least 30 minutes and up to 1 day before using, or freeze for up to 1 month.

CLARIFIED BUTTER

INGREDIENTS
1 cup unsalted butter

Makes about ⅔ cup

Melt the butter in a small, heavy saucepan over medium-low heat, watching closely to avoid burning. When the butter has fully melted and starts to bubble, reduce the heat to low and cook for about 1 minute. Remove from the heat and let stand for about 2 minutes, to allow the milk solid to settle to the bottom of the pan.

Using a spoon, skim off and discard the foam from the surface, then carefully pour off the clear yellow liquid, which is the butterfat, into a clean container. Discard the milky solids and water left behind in the pan. Use the clarified butter right away, or cover tightly for storing. Store in the refrigerator for up to 1 month. Gently warm over low heat before using.

INDEX

CREDITS

CHARLES M. SCHULZ is the artist for all strips, panels, and excerpts appearing in this book, unless otherwise cited.

PEANUTS WORLDWIDE: Endpapers; front cover (left); pages 60, 88, 90, 91, 93, 111, 128

CHARLES M. SCHULZ CREATIVE ASSOCIATES: Back cover; spine; pages 4–5, 10–11 (left), 15 (bottom left), 42, 53, 58–59 (left), 61 (bottom right), 65, 68, 69, 72, 95, 107, 122 (bottom left)

ROBERT POPE: Front cover; pages 14, 24, 27, 50, 57, 71, 75, 76, 98, 108

SCOTT JERALDS: pages 20, 23, 30, 47, 82, 87, 94, 97, 114, 117

weldon**owen**

Weldon Owen International
1045 Sansome Street
San Francisco, CA 94111
www.weldonowen.com

Library of Congress Cataloging-in-Publication data is available.

ISBN: 978-1-68188-447-9
Printed in China
10 9 8 7 6 5
2022 2023 2024 2025

President & Publisher Roger Shaw
Associate Publisher Amy Marr
Senior Editor Lisa Atwood
Production Director Tarji Rodriquez
Production Manager Binh Au

Weldon Owen would like to thank Charles M. Schulz for bringing
laughter to so many. Heartfelt thanks also to all the folks at Cameron
+ Company who have worked with such wonderful creativity and
diligence in producing this book.

Produced in conjunction with Cameron + Company
Publisher Chris Gruener
Creative Director Iain Morris
Designer Amy Wheless
Managing Editor Jan Hughes

Cameron + Company would first and foremost like to thank Charles
M. Schulz for bringing *Peanuts* into the world. We would also like
to thank Peanuts Worldwide LLC and Charles M. Schulz Creative
Associates for keeping his legacy alive and for their help in making this
book possible—special thanks to Senior Editor Alexis E. Fajardo for his
tireless efforts on this project. A resounding thank-you to Roger Shaw
and Lisa Atwood at Weldon Owen, for making this book possible.